# Mary, Mary

Mary, Mary, quite contrary,
How does your garden grow?
With silver bells
And cockle shells,
And pretty maids all in a row.

# Activity 1

## The school grounds

Say the rhyme.

Can you remember the plants which grow in the school grounds?

* What do these plants look like?
* Where are they growing?
* Why are they not there all the time?

Go outside into the school grounds.

Play I-spy.

**Collect**

living things    non-living things

Take care to protect living things.

**You will need**

magnifying glasses

Look at the living things through magnifying glasses.

# Designing and making Mary's garden

**You will need**

collection of living things

containers

stones

digging tools

Let's design a garden for Mary.
Decide what to put in the garden.

Choose a garden container.
* What shape do you want it to be?
* Do you want a shallow one or a deep one?

Put soil into the container.
* Do you want the soil to be dusty or muddy and wet?

You could try putting stepping stones in the garden for Mary to walk on.
* Do you want large stones or small stones?

Is your garden beautiful?
Is your garden useful?
Who is the garden for? Who is Mary?

## Talking about our gardens

Can you remember how you made your garden?
Talk about how you made your garden to the others in your class.

* Who is the garden for?
* What kind of person needs a garden?
* What kind of things grow in the garden?
* How do we keep the garden looking pretty?

# Pretty maids all in a row

## Collect

 artificial flowers

Some people use artificial flowers to decorate rooms.
Why are artificial flowers, artificial?

Arrange some artificial flowers in a vase.
Do you think they look attractive?

Some people like artificial flowers.
Some people don't like artificial flowers.

Make a chart showing which flowers people like. Real or artificial.

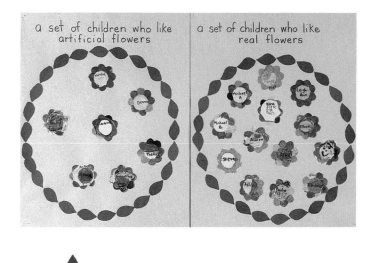

# Activity 5

## Making paper flowers

**You will need**

tape

garden ties

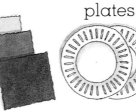
tissue paper

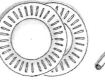
plates

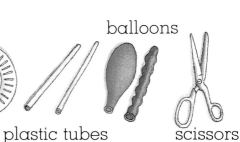
balloons

plastic tubes

scissors

Make some paper flowers.

**1** Tie a balloon onto the end of a piece of plastic tubing using garden ties.

**2** Cut some tissue paper into a circle. Use a plate as a guide. Use different colours of tissue paper.

**3** Put several tissue layers together. Make a hole in the centre and push the plastic tube through. Wrap the tissues around the tube with tape.

**4** Blow the balloon up through the tube.

# Pneumatics!

What happens to the paper flowers when you blow through the plastic tube?

How do the flowers work? Why do they work?

＊Which flower opened the most?
＊Which flower opened the least?

How could you improve the flowers?

Play with the flowers.

# Finding out about pneumatics

Moving balloons.

**You will need**

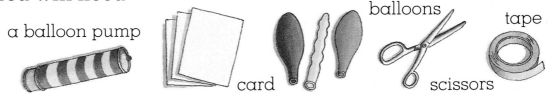

a balloon pump

card

balloons

scissors

tape

Blow up a balloon and then release it. Watch it.

* Where does it go?
* What does it do?
* Why does it move at all?
* Where does it get its energy from?
* What kind of changes do you notice in the balloon as it moves forwards, upwards and downwards?
* When does the air start to come out?
* In which direction does the air go as the balloon moves?

Can you make the balloon go straight across the room?

# Pneumatics all around us

Air is very useful for making things work.

Can you think of any inventions which use air?

paddling pool

bike tyres

**You will need**

bicycle pump

a bicycle

inflatable
paddling pool

foot pump

Let the teacher pump up a bicycle tyre.
Feel the different pressures of the air in the tyre:

＊ before the tyre was pumped up.
＊ after the tyre was pumped up.
＊ What differences do you feel?

Help the teacher
pump up a paddling
pool using a foot
pump.

How do foot pumps
work?

# A tinkering table

We know that some things work by using air.

**Collect**

Toys which move using different kinds of energy.

Put your toys on a tinkering table.
Try and discover how different toys work.

# Our magic garden

What else can you think of to put in your magic garden?
You could make a tree.

**You will need**

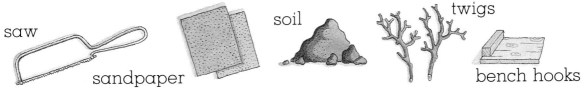

saw
sandpaper
soil
twigs
bench hooks

Collect some interesting looking twigs which you could use for trees.

✳ What different shapes can you find?
✳ How does the wood feel?

Choose the best twig for size.
Choose the best twig for shape.

Shape your tree.
Use sandpaper to smooth the wood.
Use a saw and bench hooks to cut the wood to the right shape.

Put your tree in the garden.

## Light up your tree

Some people like lights on their trees.

Do you know anyone who has a light on their tree?

Do you want to put lights on your tree?

First of all, you need to find out about electricity.

A Christmas tree uses lights

### Electricity
**You will need**

two wires  a battery 4.5v  a torch bulb 3.5v a bulb holder

Let your teacher set up an electrical circuit.

Do not play with electricity unless you use a battery or when an adult provides train sets.

**Be careful** ⚠

Can you find a way of making the bulb light up?

# Decorating your trees with lights

## You will need

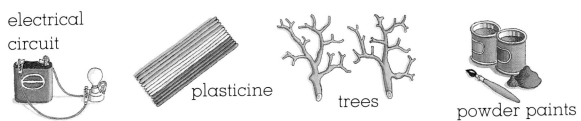

electrical circuit

plasticine

trees

powder paints

Look at the electricity circuit.

Can you put more than one light in the circuit?

Can you make the two lights shine as brightly as one light?

You can paint over the bulbs with different colours of powder paints to make the lights pretty and attractive.

Decorate your trees with the lights.

# Arranging your garden

Design and make your garden.

Make your garden look pretty and attractive.
Do you think you could improve on it?
Do you want to move the tree?
Do you want to move the path?

Show your garden to the rest of your class. Tell everyone who it is for and why it is needed.

Play with your magic garden.

Paint a picture of it.

Write a short story about your garden.

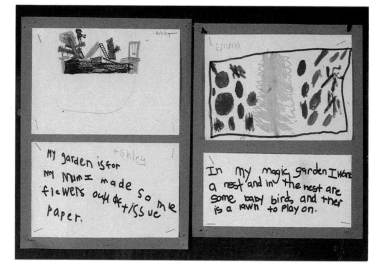

My garden is for my Mum I made some flewers ouh of tissue paper.

In my magic garden I want a nest and in the nest are some baby birds and ther is a lawn to play on.

# Technology is about helping people

Let's grow our own gardens which we can give or sell to people.

*This market garden grows and sells lettuces.*

### You will need

mustard seeds

yoghurt cartons

orange peel

cress seeds   containers         sand    blotting         sawdust

paper

What size of container will you need to grow your seeds?
Search for containers you could use.

Grow things on different materials.
Try sand, felt, blotting paper.

# Activity 15

## Testing your gardens

Look at your gardens daily.

When the gardens have grown, sort the gardens into ones which worked and ones which didn't work.

Why did some gardens work and not others?

How can you improve on your results?

◆ Keep the container the same but change the material you grow your seeds in. Give each one the same amount of water.

◆ Keep the material the same but change the container.

Find the best way to grow your seeds. Give your seeds away or sell them at the next school fete.